The Special

Wild Flowers of

The Isle of Purbeck

The Rev. Edward Pratt

ISBN 978-0-9567791-0-6

Designed, published and distributed by
The Rev. Edward Pratt,
7 Bay Close, Swanage, Dorset, BH19 1RE

Photographs by the author

Printed by Henry Ling Limited,
The Dorset Press, Dorchester, DT1 1HD

Cover: Early Spider Orchid

Introduction

The Isle of Purbeck is the richest area for its size in Great Britain for native and anciently introduced wild flowers. This is, firstly, because so many different geological layers, together with the varied coastline, give rise to a wide variety of habitats – down, heath, grassland, stream, riverside, bog, pond, wood, cliff, dune, shingle, saltmarsh etc., and secondly because of its situation halfway along the south coast, where the ranges of eastern and western species overlap.

This booklet is designed to enhance your leisure time or holiday, by introducing you to the special flowers of the area, and showing you when and where to see them. The species in this booklet are special because of the limited number of sites where they occur in Britain.

The flowering times chart on pages 7 and 8 shows, at a glance, which months the different species are in flower. A selection of sites across "The Isle" is given for each species in the Plant List beginning on page 9 – but many of them can be found in other locations too. When you visit the sites given, you will no doubt see other interesting species.

Over half of the plants in this booklet are illustrated; you will need an identification book for the others. Two of the best books are *The Wild Flower Key* by Rose and O'Reilly (Warne, 2006) and *Collins Flower Guide* by Streeter (Collins, 2009). Grasses, sedges, ferns and fern allies and other less colourful specialities have not been included in this booklet.

For a full account of the locations of all the less common species in the area, where they are accessible to the public, see the author's *The Wild Flowers of The Isle of Purbeck, Brownsea and Sandbanks* (Brambleby Books, 2008). That book also contains useful information about looking for wild flowers, descriptions of flower-rich locations in the area, a calendar of special sights, suggestions for walks, and much else.

About the Plant List

The **species**, and a few hybrids, are listed in the order in which they occur in most current identification books. The scientific names used are those in *New Flora of The British Isles* by Stace (Cambridge, Third edition, 2010).

About half the species included in this booklet have an official designation as to their scarcity, as follows –

Nationally Rare species have occurred in only 1 to 15 (out of about 2500) Ten Kilometre National Grid squares (hectads) in Great Britain since 1987.

Nationally Scarce species have occurred in only 16 to 100 hectads nationally since the same date.

Dorset Rare species have been found in 3 or fewer sites in the county since 1990, and are not in the previous two categories.

Dorset Scarce species have been found in 4 to 10 sites in Dorset since the same date, and are also not nationally rare or scarce.

The other species included in this booklet occur in less than 500 hectads in Great Britain.

Hairy-fruited Cornsalad, a species with very small pale pink or mauve flowers – a National Rarity, which has its "headquarters" in Purbeck – *see page 30.*

Tufted Centaury, on the right, another of our special plants – see page 23. The smaller pale pink flowers, with four lobes, on the left, are Squinancywort, a Bedstraw.

The **photographs** in the Plant List are above, alongside, or, when stated, below the species. When there is no photograph, there are usually some notes to help with identification. When a species may be confused with a near relative, the differences are given. Occasionally, use of a lens is suggested. 10 times magnification lenses are often stocked by opticians and are not expensive. Viewing a plant through reversed binoculars may suffice in some cases.

The **sites** are listed from west to east, using place-names on the Ordnance Survey 1:25.000 Explorer map OL15, 2004 or later editions. This map also gives routes of public paths and bridleways in relation to field boundaries, and shows open access areas in pale yellow. Each site begins with the nearest town or village. The villages of Corfe Castle, Langton Matravers and Worth Matravers are abbreviated to Corfe, Langton and Worth, as is done locally. Some of the villages are quite small; you might like to locate West Holme (in the W), Steeple (in the SW), and Arne (in the N) at an early stage.

The Tyneham area within the Army Ranges is open most weekends and in holiday periods. There are two areas near Swanage called "Round Down" – at Ulwell and at Durlston; the text makes clear which is intended. When there are two or more sites given near the same village, the sites are separated by a semi-colon. Occasional reference is made to the Easting lines; these are the National Grid vertical blue lines, numbered along the top and bottom of the map. Sharford Bridge, Strip Lynchets and Corfe Castle are written in ancient script on the map; that is not done in this booklet.

Enjoy yourself

The Isle of Purbeck is a great place to relax on holiday, leaving your work and other pressures behind. Finding beautiful wild flowers will be a joy, and those that are rare or scarce especially so. Enjoy yourself!

Please do not pick wild flowers, except small parts for identification – take their photograph, taking care not to crush other flowers. Picking any part of Early Gentian, Vipersgrass and Early Spider Orchid is against the law. Sadly, there are a few people who dig up orchids. This is why our rarer orchids are not included in this booklet. Digging orchids is not only illegal and selfish, but foolish, as they are unlikely to survive transplanting.

About the author

He has been studying wild flowers in his spare time for 35 years. He retired to Swanage in 1997, and is a botanical volunteer for The National Trust, Durlston Country Park, The Dorset Wildlife Trust and the RSPB. He also leads wild flower walks. He is a founder member of The Dorset Flora Group.

Acknowledgments

The author is most grateful to David Leadbetter and John Wright for kindly reading the text and making helpful suggestions, to his son Jonathan for advice on colouring in the flowering times chart, and to Henry Ling Limited for advice and for printing the booklet.

Main flowering times

Species	April	May	June	July	Aug.	Sept.
Small-flower'd Buttercup	▓	▓				
Shrubby Sea-blite				▓	▓	
Prickly Saltwort				▓	▓	
Dwarf Mouse-ear	▓	▓				
Nottingham Catchfly		▓	▓			
Pale St. John's Wort				▓	▓	
Godlingston Sundew				▓	▓	▓
Great Sundew				▓	▓	▓
Round-l'd x Gt Sundew				▓	▓	▓
Pale Dog Violet		▓	▓			
Wild Cabbage	▓	▓				
Dorset Heath				▓	▓	▓
Dorset Hybrid Heath			▓	▓	▓	▓
Mossy Stonecrop	▓	▓	▓			
Fragrant Agrimony				▓	▓	
Wild Pear	▓					
Sainfoin		▓	▓	▓	▓	
Hairy Birdsfoot Trefoil			▓	▓		
Slender Tare			▓	▓		
Narrow-l'ed Everl'g Pea				▓	▓	
Grass Vetchling			▓	▓		
Yellow Vetchling			▓	▓		
Clustered Clover			▓	▓		
Suffocated Clover	▓	▓	▓	▓		
Stars-in-grass			▓	▓		
Broad-leaved Spurge			▓	▓	▓	▓
Portland Spurge	▓	▓	▓	▓	▓	▓
Pale Flax		▓	▓			
Shepherd's Needle	▓	▓				
Chalk Milkwort	▓	▓				
Corky-f'd Water-dropw't			▓	▓	▓	

Species	April	May	June	July	Aug.	Sept.
Corn Parsley				■	■	■
Knotted Hedge Parsley		■	■	■		
Yellow Centaury				■	■	
Tufted Centaury				■	■	
Early Gentian	■	■	■			
Marsh Gentian					■	■
Sea Bindweed			■	■	■	
Dodder			■	■	■	
Common Gromwell		■	■			
Houndstongue		■	■	■		
White Horehound			■	■	■	■
Common Calamint			■	■	■	■
English Sticky Eyebright			■	■	■	
Broad-leaved Eyebright		■	■	■	■	
Yellow Bartsia			■	■	■	■
Toothwort	■	■				
Ivy Broomrape			■	■	■	
Pale Butterwort			■	■	■	■
Nordic Bladderwort				■	■	■
Nettle-l'd Bellflower				■	■	■
Hairy-fruited Cornsalad		■				
Wild Madder			■	■	■	
Woolly Thistle			■	■	■	
Vipersgrass		■	■	■		
Small Cudweed		■	■	■	■	
Golden Samphire				■	■	■
Chamomile			■	■	■	■
Lesser Water-plantain		■	■	■	■	■
Italian Lords-and-ladies		■				
Marsh Helleborine				■	■	
Autumn Lady's Tresses					■	■
Early Marsh Orchid			■			
Early Spider Orchid	■	■				
Wasp Orchid			■			

8

Plant List

Small-flowered Buttercup *Ranunculus parviflorus*
April to May.
It grows close to the ground in short grass; the inconspicuous flowers usually have only one or two narrow petals, as in the photo above, not five as painted in some books!
Steeple: here and there on the down slope N of village. **Church Knowle:** E end of Ridgeway Hill. **Worth:** here and there on E side of valley up to 200m N of Renscombe Farm. **Langton:** along top of slope N of Dancing Ledge. **Swanage:** E of Durlston Visitor Centre; here and there near bottom of S side of Ballard Down. Plentiful at all sites.

Shrubby Sea-blite *Suaeda vera*
July to October. *Nationally Scarce.*
Young plants can look like Annual Sea-blite, but the leaf-tips are blunt, whereas in Annual Sea-blite they are acute.
Studland: neck of Redhorn Quay peninsular; NW-facing shore of bay just E of Redhorn Quay; plentiful on sandy spit 400m NE of Redhorn Quay.

Prickly Saltwort *Salsola kali* subsp. *kali*
July to September. *Dorset Scarce.*
Green flowers. After a decline, it has happily increased in recent years.
Studland: 3.5Km N of village from middle to SE end of Shell Bay - plentiful.

Dwarf Mouse-ear *Cerastium pumilum*
Late April to May. *Nationally Scarce.* **Photo below left.**
This species always has five petals, which are usually slightly longer than the sepals; its lower leaves are often somewhat crimson; it comes into flower later than Sea Mouse-ear (*Cerastium diffusum*), which sometimes grows nearby and usually has four petals, but sometimes five. The number of plants depends on the weather; in a dry spring there may be almost none.
Swanage: here and there along brow of Round Down in Durlston Country Park; in Townsend Nature Reserve in at least twelve places in short grass and on anthills and banks.

Nottingham Catchfly *Silene nutans*
Mid-May to mid-June. *Nationally Scarce.*
The petals curl inward in daytime. **Photo above right.**
Swanage: scattered in rough grassland near Coast Path on Ballard Down from 200 to 350m E of triangulation pillar.

Pale St. John's Wort
Hypericum montanum
July to mid-August.
Dorset Scarce.
Always just a few plants. Flowers
cluster together at the top of the stem.
Church Knowle: among low bushes
on Stonehill Down Nature Reserve W
of top W corner of largest quarry.
Corfe: E of 75th to 85th steps up East
Hill; by Purbeck Way here and there
250 to 450m E of junction with road
near Challow Farm.

**Godlingston Sundew (Round-leaved and Oblong-leaved Sundew
hybrid)** *Drosera* x *belezeana* (*D. rotundifolia* x *intermedia*)
July to September (leaves from June).
Usually easily recognisable by leaf shape and masses of leaves pointing
upwards. Godlingston Heath may be its only site in Europe.
Studland: plentiful 60m W of the Agglestone (there are eleven other
small sites on Godlingston Heath).

11

Great Sundew *Drosera anglica*
July to September (leaves from June). *Dorset Scarce.*
Long leaves, gradually widening. Its flowers are 10 to 13mm across
when open in morning sun.
Stoborough: in area just E of Easting line 95 in Hartland Moor National
Nature Reserve, 250m N of boundary line on top of high ground in
middle of Reserve. **Studland:** in centre of bog E of Ferry Road opposite
bridleway to Greenlands.

**Round-leaved and
Great Sundew hybrid**
Drosera x *obovata*
(*D. rotundifolia* x *anglica*)
July to September (leaves from
June).
Leaves intermediate between
those of its parents, but they
can vary in shape on the same
plant. Flowers 8 to 10mm across
when open in morning sun.
Stoborough and **Studland:**
small numbers in same areas
as species next above.

Pale Dog Violet *Viola lactea*
May to June. *Nationally Scarce.*
The petals are pale mauve. Some leaf-bases taper into their stalk, others
meet it at right angles, but none have heart-shaped bases.
Stoborough: on Stoborough Heath by Purbeck Way from about the
bottom of the "S" of Stoborough Heath on the map to the top of the "d"
of Stocks Wood; by Dismantled Tramway 150 to 300m N of A351.

Wild Cabbage *Brassica oleracea*
Mid-April to June. *Nationally Scarce.*
The ancestor of cultivated Cabbages, Brussels Sprouts, Broccoli,
Cauliflower, Kale and Kohl-rabi!
Worth & Langton: here and there from Seacombe Cliff to Dancing
Ledge. **Studland:** near cliff-top from Ballard Point to Handfast Point.

Dorset Heath *Erica ciliaris*
Mid-July to October. *Nationally Rare.* **See photo on back cover.**
The County Flower. Its flowers are usually down one side of the stem;
occasionally they are grouped together at the top, like the hybrid below.
Stoborough: plentiful by and to W of N end of Soldiers Road; plentiful
in damp areas on Hartland Moor National Nature Reserve. **Arne:**
plentiful on triangular road junction 2Km SW of village. **Studland:** few
NW of bog E of Ferry Road opposite bridleway to Greenlands. **Other
sites:** shared with the hybrid below.

Dorset Hybrid Heath (Dorset Heath and Cross-leaved Heath hybrid)
Erica x *watsonii* (*E. ciliaris* x *tetralix*)
Late June to October.
Its flowers are clustered like Cross-leaved Heath, but they are larger and deeper pink. To identify this hybrid correctly, open a floret and look at the pollen-bearing anthers with a lens. Cross-leaved Heath anthers have backward-pointing pale appendages, nearly as long as the anthers themselves. Dorset Heath anthers have no appendages. Hybrid Heath anthers have brown appendages less than half as long as the anthers; these can be seen on fresh flowers in late June right through the winter to the following June, when they have long been shrivelled (as on the left in the photo). When the plants are mature they form domed humps, which can be picked out at some distance, with experience.
Stoborough: plentiful in large area to W of N end of Soldiers Road; on E side of Soldiers Road 40m from N end; many large plants along N side of Hartland Moor, and elsewhere on Moor. **Arne:** scattered on W end of Coombe Heath 100m SE of Arne Road. **Studland:** about 150m NE of Agglestone scattered W of path along S side of E-W valley.

Mossy Stonecrop *Crassula tillaea*
April to mid-June. *Nationally Scarce.*
Its foliage starts green, and then turns bright red in May, as in the photo.
Its flowers are very small – lens needed.
Corfe: 2.5Km N of village on SW/NE-running part of bridleway W of
Sharford Bridge 150 to 200m along that bridleway from the road. **Arne:**
N of Shipstal viewpoint 5m S of bridleway; on E part of viewpoint itself.
Studland: 300 to 400m N of Visitor Centre here and there E of path
locally signed "Heather Walk"; 3.5Km N of village on level bank above
shore 50, 150 and 175m SW of Gravel Point.

Fragrant Agrimony *Agrimonia procera*
June to September.
It is distinguished from Agrimony (*Agrimonia eupatoria)* by the slightly
backward direction of some bristles on the fruit, by smell, and by
numerous tiny stalkless glands under the leaves (use lens).
Stoborough: scattered along 100m of S end of Soldiers Road on both
sides; plentiful on W side of same road 350-500m from S end. **Corfe:**
2Km N of village on W side of road to Slepe 200m N of corner near
Scotland. **Studland:** on NE side of bridleway to Greenlands 325m from
Ferry Road.

Wild Pear *Pyrus pyraster*
Late April.
This genuine Wild Pear has thorns. Most pear trees in the countryside are the cultivated species *Pyrus communis*. Wild Pear only bears a few fruit occasionally, because of lack of neighbours with which to cross-pollinate; the fruit are only slightly pear-shaped.
Stoborough: N edge of lay-by on N side of Holme Lane 500m W of Springfield Hotel at E end of Lane.

Sainfoin *Onobrychis viciifolia*
Mid-May to June.
Like miniature pink Lupins.
Worth: by Coast Path both 225m N of Emmetts Hill and 600m E of St. Aldhelm's Head Lookout Station. **Swanage:** W of path which runs from Townsend Reserve towards Round Down 25 and 140m S of where it leaves Reserve (plentiful at latter site); in large field W of Durlston Visitor Centre 20m NE of small wood in SW corner.

Hairy Birdsfoot Trefoil *Lotus subbiflorus*
Mid-May to August. *Nationally Scarce*
The flowers are <u>much</u> smaller than the common Birdsfoot Trefoil; plants are very hairy. Not found at all sites every year.
Corfe: few NW of village on broad verge on NE side of A351 roundabout. **Studland:** N side of National Trust approach road to Visitor Centre just W of coach park; few 3.5Km N of village in NW corner of Shell Bay car park.

Slender Tare *Vicia parviflora*
June to mid-July. *Nationally Scarce.*
It often has three or four flowers together 8 to 9mm long, whereas its close relative Smooth Tare has one or two flowers together 4 to 8mm long. Five seeds can be seen as bumps in Slender Tare's pods, whereas Smooth Tare usually has 4 (or 3).
Worth: here and there NW of Seacombe Quarry both by rocks by Coast Path and on the down; scattered in SE part of field N of Seacombe Cliff.
Swanage: near S end of path on W side of Durlston Country Park's Centenary Meadow (ask at Visitor Centre for directions).

Narrow-leaved Everlasting Pea *Lathyrus sylvestris*
June to August. *Dorset Scarce.* **Photo below left.**
Kimmeridge: 80m E of T-junction NE of Kimmeridge village on N side of road to Bradle Farm.

Yellow Vetchling *Lathyrus aphaca*
June to July. *Nationally Scarce.* **Photo above right.**
It is an annual species, so some sites change from year to year. It has grey-green foliage and the flowers are borne singly; in contrast to the common yellow-flowered species, Meadow Vetchling, which has deep green foliage and its flowers in clusters.
Swanage: in several places on the edge of meadows and by gateways in Durlston Country Park, including gateway 100m SW of Visitor Centre.

Grass Vetchling *Lathyrus nissolia*
Mid-June to early July.
It is an annual species, so it varies in quantity from year to year. The plants are not noticed until they flower; these rubies in the grass then look delightful. They have a short flowering period in dry seasons.
Worth: here and there on SW part of down NW of Seacombe Quarry; by Coast Path along SE edge of same Down 100m S of top of steps; by Coast Path half way along field above Seacombe Cliff. **Swanage:** several sites by paths around the edges of the four meadows running W-wards from Durlston Visitor Centre.

Suffocated Clover *Trifolium suffocatum*
April to July (and August in wet years). *Nationally Scarce.*
The tiny off-white flowers are almost hidden inside their clustered sepal-tubes (use a lens). Plants are best found by learning to recognise the light green rosette of the leaves.
Corfe: 2.5Km N of village in shallow ruts of grassy track W of gate NW of small wood NW of Sharford Bridge (with other clovers). **Studland:** between car park rows both N and S of tree-covered mound in centre of car park nearest Redend Point (Middle Beach car park).

Clustered Clover *Trifolium glomeratum*
Late May to June. *Nationally Scarce.*
Hairless or almost so. Small clusters of flowers grow along stems. It may
not show if the spring has been dry.
Corfe: 2.5Km N of village on SW/NE-running part of bridleway W of
Sharford Bridge 50m along bridleway from road. **Arne:** on partly bare
ground in N end of triangular field SW of car park 10m from kissing-
gate S-wards (this field is a reserve car park at busy times). **Studland:** S-
facing bank just W of Visitor Centre toilets; 3.5Km N of village E of
small roundabout at Shell Bay.

Stars-in-grass, Bastard Toadflax *Thesium humifusum*
June to August. *Nationally Scarce.*
Quite unlike Toadflaxes, except perhaps when in young leaf and very
small. It is deserving and worthy of its new name: Stars-in-grass.
Steeple: on the down N of village from 80 to 120m E of bend in zigzag
bridleway from bottom of the down upwards for 20m (plentiful in some
years). **Corfe:** scattered on the down N of Purbeck Way 150m W of
radio mast on Rollington Hill. **Worth:** on the down towards S tip of
large field S of Eastington Farm. **Swanage:** several places in Townsend
Nature Reserve including 90m SE of NW entrance; in Lighthouse Field
in Durlston Country Park between Mile Indicator Posts.

Broad-leaved Spurge *Euphorbia platyphyllos*
June to October. *Dorset Scarce.*
There are rounded deep yellow glands in the flowers, similar to those of
Sun Spurge, but the leaf-bases are heart-shaped rather than tapered, and
its fruits have warts rather than being nearly smooth (use lens).
Kingston: here and there along 500m by S side of road W of village
beyond W edge of The Plantation wood.

Portland Spurge *Euphorbia portlandica*
April to August.
The deep yellow flower-glands have horns – as in photo above. The
leaves are fleshy, with prominent midribs underneath them.
Tyneham: visible but unreachable on SW corner of Worbarrow Tout -
from top of Tout descend path on SW side, use binoculars before path
gets too narrow for safety. **Swanage:** here and there by narrow climbers'
path above cliff-top (S of Coast Path) 200 to 400 m W of lighthouse
(take care); base of chalk cliffs on N side of Swanage Bay 150m E of W
end of chalk.

Pale Flax *Linum bienne*
Mid-May to July.
As many of its flowers drop their petals around midday, they need to be
seen in their glory in the morning.
West Holme: scattered along NW side of B3070 crossing West Holme
Heath 375 to 550m SW of crossroads. **Worth & Langton:** plentiful on
some slopes above Coast Path from Seacombe Cliff eastwards.
Swanage: plentiful in meadows in Durlston Country Park.

Chalk Milkwort *Polygala calcarea*
April to June.
The inner sepals are <u>bright</u> blue, pink or white, with one or no loops in
the veins each side of the central vein (use lens); this can still be seen
when the sepals have turned green. Its stems are usually upright, with a
rosette of leaves down below in the grass. In contrast Common
Milkwort, which grows in similar places, has its inner sepals <u>dull</u> blue,
purple or white, with several veins making loops, which also can still be
seen when sepals have turned green. Common Milkwort's stems are
usually slanting, and there is normally no rosette of leaves below.
Langton: in E side of the coastal field E of the field above Dancing
Ledge. **Swanage:** S-facing slope of N arm of E end of Godlingston Hill
200 to 400m W of road; beautiful patches by road to lighthouse and on
brow of Round Down in Durlston Country Park.

Shepherd's Needle *Scandix pecten-veneris*
April to May. *Dorset Rare.*
It has long fruits – like thick needles.
Worth: S side of Coast Path in two patches 600m E of the Lookout
Station on St. Aldhelm's Head.

Corky-fruited Water-dropwort *Oenanthe pimpinelloides*
June to early August.
The flowers are always white, not pink, in Britain; its stems are narrowly
hollow, except for the lowest and highest sections which are solid late in
their season; its flowers press together when in seed; the fruit shape,
rather than its tiny corky base, is a distinctive feature.
Corfe: plentiful immediately S of village in corner of Corfe Common
just NE of A351; N side of road opposite Higher Bushey Farm.
Langton: plentiful on both sides of path in meadow S of Spyway Barn.
Swanage: many in several meadows in Durlston Country Park.

Corn Parsley *Petroselinum segetum*
July to September.
Difficult to spot; the tiny flowers and grey-green leaves and stems are
inconspicuous, despite its moderate height. Lower leaves have 4 to 12
pairs of leaflets; stalks of umbels and of flowers are very unequal. Smells
like Parsley.
Worth: very plentiful by and below spring towards SW corner of down
W of Seacombe Quarry; near track 60m SE of stile W of Eastington
Farm; near SE corner of large field S of Eastington Farm; by coast fence
110m E of SW corner of field above Seacombe Cliff. **Swanage:** on bank
just W of SW corner of Durlston car park.

Knotted Hedge Parsley *Torilis nodosa*
Mid-May to July. **Photo on opposite page.**
Inconspicuous low species.
Tyneham: plentiful beside Army Range path for over 300m when
approaching Tyneham Cap from E. **Church Knowle:** near steps at
church gate. **Worth:** fringing Coast Path 350-650m E of St. Aldhelm's
Head Lookout Station; in field above Seacombe Cliff both along S part
of W wall, and here and there near Coast Path. **Langton:** in field east of
that above Dancing Ledge along 40m of Coast Path fence in SW corner
of field. **Swanage:** by kerbs of W car park at Durlston Country Park.

Yellow Centaury *Cicendia filiformis*
Late June to July. *Nationally Scarce.*
The tiny flowers, 2 to 4mm across, are difficult to spot; they only open in the mornings and in full sun. Numbers vary greatly from year to year according to the weather and the openness of ground.
Stoborough: on N end of Stoborough Heath on SW side of path which runs SE from S of Springfield Hotel from 260 to 300m from NW end of the path. **Corfe:** 2Km NE of village on S side of public path which runs along S edge of Wytch Heath (Forest) – 190, 290, 320 and 410m W of road. **Studland:** in field SE of covered Reservoir NW of village 15m SE of N gateway into field from NE/SW-running bridleway.

Tufted Centaury *Centaurium erythraea* var. *capitatum*
Late June to early August. **See photo on page 5.**
The stamens of each flower are joined to the petal-tube near its base, rather than near the top of the petal-tube as in Common Centaury (use lens). Plants are only up to 1.5cm high, almost flat on ground, usually little larger than a 50pence piece. Ignore plants 2cm or more in height with stalks that can be seen – those will be small specimens of Common Centaury.
Swanage: scattered in field W of Anvil Point lighthouse in an arc SE-S-SW-W-NW-N around the knoll 50m W of NW corner of the lighthouse enclosure; 60m NW of same enclosure corner on NE side of tarmac path; 15m SE of SE corner of the lighthouse enclosure.

Early Gentian *Gentianella anglica*
Mid-April to early June, peaking last week of May. *Nationally Scarce.*
Photo below left. Its flowers are purple, with four or five petal-lobes,
opening in the sun; when closed they can be difficult to spot. The number
of plants varies considerably from year to year.
Worth: SW-facing slope of field S of Eastington Farm 150m E of SW
corner of field. **Langton:** W end of the field W of Dancing Ledge 30m
NE of Coast Path gate; 30m SW of NE corner of same field. **Swanage:**
in Durlston Country Park both 30m NW of the lighthouse enclosure on
SW side of road, and on bank between Mile Indicator Posts; here and
there on N side of Purbeck Way on Ballard Down 400 to 700m E of gate
to the down above Whitecliff Farm.

Marsh Gentian *Gentiana pneumonanthe*
Mid-August to early October. *Nationally Scarce.* **Photo above right.**
The chief glory of wet heaths, not marshes! No photo does it justice.
Stoborough: in area 600m N of S end of Dismantled Tramway 50m W
of tramway; here and there on N side of Hartland Moor especially 75m
NW of most NE pool shown on the Moor. **Corfe:** 2.5Km E of village
near NW corner of square-shaped open access heath W of Rempstone
Farm. **Studland:** 130m NW of Puckstone; around bog E of Ferry Road
opposite bridleway to Greenlands – 190 to 220m SE of entrance is best.

24

Sea Bindweed *Calystegia soldanella*
June to August. *Dorset Scarce.*
Note the fleshy leaves.
Studland: just beyond areas of fenced fore-dunes 375m N of Visitor
Centre and continuing for 175m N-wards; 3.5Km N of village 30m N of
E end of boardwalk from Shell Bay car park NW-wards for 50m.

Dodder *Cuscuta epithymum*
June to July.
Clusters of pink flowers on very thin wiry stems. It is parasitic on heather
and a few other plants. Numbers vary considerably year to year.
Corfe: 3.5Km N of village on S side of small triangle of open access
land just S of Slepe Farm 175 to 225m W of road. **Studland:** 3.5Km N
of village E of Ferry Road from Shell Bay car park SW-wards for 425m
from 5m to 100m E of road.

Common Gromwell *Lithospermum officinale*
Late May to July.
Small, off-white flowers.
Swanage: N of Ulwell near steps on path up the down to the Obelisk;
few by Purbeck Way NE of Ulwell.

Houndstongue *Cynoglossum officinale*
Mid-May to mid-July.
Small, deep crimson flowers.
Steeple: here and there on the down N of village, especially near rabbit holes. **Langton:** here and there along the tops of the fields which slope down to the cliffs. **Swanage:** plentiful near SE corner of Round Down at Ulwell; here and there on Ballard Down, especially near steepest part of the bridleway N of Whitecliff Farm, and in the shallow coombe crossed by the Purbeck Way 400m NE of the gate on the previous bridleway.

Common Calamint *Clinopodium ascendens*
July to September.
The flowers are in loose, not densely hairy, whorls. The two lower teeth of the sepal-tubes are longer than the three others.
Stoborough: here and there on NE side of bypass from 20 to 120m SE of path which runs W-wards from village centre. **Corfe:** plentiful here and there inside castle; much on S slopes outside castle walls (if not grazed), including near stream bridge on road to Church Knowle W of castle. **Swanage:** near stepped path from Ulwell to Obelisk, with relatives Wild Basil and Wild Marjoram; various other sites near scrub on Ballard Down.

White Horehound *Marrubium vulgare*
June to July. *Nationally Scarce*
Somewhat mealy leaves and small white flowers.
Worth: by Coast Path at Emmetts Hill mainly 130m N of steps.

English Sticky Eyebright *Euphrasia officinalis* subsp. *anglica*
June to August. *Dorset Scarce.*
This is the easiest species of Eyebright to identify: it is covered with
hairs which have tiny glands on their ends. The hairs are at least 6 times
the length of the glands (use lens). It is the only species of Eyebright in
this area which has this gland/hair length ratio. The leaves are light
green. (There are four other species of Eyebright in Purbeck, all of them
more widespread.)
Corfe: plentiful on higher ground of Corfe Common SW of the valley
for up to 150m on both sides of the route with public access (green-
dotted on map) which crosses the western side of the Common. Little
Kneeling Eyebright (*Euphrasia confusa*) is sometimes nearby, flowering
from July, with few hairs, and darker green leaves.

Broad-leaved Eyebright *Euphrasia tetraquetra*
May to August.
The leaves are longer than the lengths between them on the stem; and the
earliest flowers are low on the stem. It begins flowering in May, before
other Eyebrights.
Corfe: N side of Purbeck Way 150 to 325m W of radio mast on
Rollington Hill. **Langton:** scattered patches in many S-facing sloping
fields above sea, especially near Coast Path. **Swanage:** scattered on S-
facing sloping fields in Durlston Country Park; plentiful on steep down
SW of Obelisk at W end of Ballard Down.

Yellow Bartsia
Parentucellia viscosa
June to September.
Stoborough: thinly scattered
in a large area W of Soldiers
Road W and SW of the name
'Slepe Heath' on map; on
Slepe Heath itself 25 to 50m
N of gate at SW corner.

Toothwort *Lathraea squamaria*
February to May (beginning late January to April according to weather).
Parasitic chiefly on Hazel, also on Field Maple and other trees.
Church Knowle: plentiful here and there near S (top) edge of woods
which are N part of Stonehill Down Nature Reserve, in some of the areas
where Ramsons (Wild Garlic) is not dominant, especially 50m and 200
to 400m E of path. **Studland:** 3Km W of village SE of bridleway
through E end of King's Wood 30m SW of E corner of wood.

Ivy Broomrape *Orobanche hederae*
Late May to July.
Stigma lobes are dull yellow. It does not occur every year at some sites.
Stoborough: S side of road 175m W of W end of Holme Lane
Plantation. **Corfe:** on left 5 to 10m beyond gatehouse to West Bailey of
castle. **Worth:** by and E of junction of Winspit path with Coast Path
(best site). **Swanage:** S of Railway Station around Health Centre (with
Common Broomrape nearby); on W side of road to Durlston opposite S-
most house; both sides of unmade W-E road S of that house 40m from
road to Durlston.

Pale Butterwort *Pinguicula lusitanica*
Late May to early September.
Inconspicuous plants, with one small pale pink flower per stem.
Arne: on S side of S part of triangular road junction 2Km SW of village
40m from E end of junction. **Corfe:** much on Corfe Common in parts of
valley running 50m E of and parallel to B3069 road and SW and W of
Purbeck Way. **Studland:** thinly scattered in NW part of bog E of Ferry
Road opposite bridleway to Greenlands.

Nordic Bladderwort *Utricularia stygia*
Mid-July to mid-September. *Dorset Rare.*
The flowers are bright yellow, on stems emerging from bog pools,
similar to, but slightly smaller than, Bladderwort (*Utricularia australis*).
Nordic Bladderwort flowers more in the Purbeck area than at any other
British site. It has two types of leaf: one without bladders, often green
(and pretty), just under the water surface, and the other with bladders and
few segments, deeper in the water; in contrast Bladderwort has only one
type of leaf.
Stoborough & Corfe: various sites spread across the bog pools of N
side of Hartland Moor, from Soldiers Road eastwards (the pools are more
accessible from the N side of the Moor than from the S). For those who
do not like bogs, it can often be seen through binoculars from the road
bridge over the stream 400m SE of Slepe Farm.

Nettle-leaved Bellflower
Campanula trachelium
July to early September.
Steeple: plentiful on SE side
of upper part of road through
Great Wood.
Church Knowle: S side of
road E of East Creech for
50m W of T-junction; W
side of road S of same
T-junction; SE side of road
beyond that as far as Quarry
(best, glorious, stretch**).**
Swanage: E side of path
from Ulwell lay-by to
obelisk, 75m from lay-by.

Hairy-fruited Cornsalad *Valerianella eriocarpa*
Mostly early May. *Nationally Rare.* **See photo on page 4.**
New sites have been discovered in the last ten years; more is now known
in Purbeck than anywhere else in Britain. Its tiny five-lobed flowers vary
in pale colour – mauve on Purbeck Limestone, pink on hard Chalk. The
capsules are usually hairy, but occasionally hairless, despite the species'
name; however, hairless capsules have not yet been found on land open
to the public in this area. Few plants appear in dry years.
Corfe: E side of castle mound (opposite columnar cypresses in the
garden on the other side of the A351), stretching from the path on the
side of the mound for 15m up the mound in an area 10m wide (late May,
pink). **Worth:** by Coast Path 300m E of St. Aldhelm's Head Lookout
Station. **Swanage:** 40m NE of horses' shed in middle of Townsend
Nature Reserve on two anthills and a bank; near foot of S slope of
Ballard Down above NE corner of second field W of Coast Path (pink).

Wild Madder *Rubia peregrina*
June to August.
Much larger, rougher and deeper green than Cleavers.
Worth: by Winspit path 50 and 150m N of Coast Path. **Langton:** by Coast Path 250m W of western Mile Indicator Posts. **Swanage:** here and there by Coast Path from above Tilly Whim Caves to Durlston Head.

Woolly Thistle *Cirsium eriophorum*
July to mid-August.
The purple points among the woolly bracts are sharp spines!
Worth: few on slopes N and NW of Renscombe Farm. **Langton:** 1.75Km SE of village along N edge of sloping field above Blackers Hole. **Swanage:** here and there on downland in Durlston Country Park, especially along N side of large field with lighthouse in it.

Vipersgrass *Scorzonera humilis*
Mid-May to mid-July. *Nationally Rare.*
A Dandelion-like flower, but with untoothed leaves.
Stoborough: site is on a closed reserve (The Moors), which can be visited by application to RSPB, Syldata, Arne, Dorset, BH20 5BJ, Tel: 01929 553360, who will give directions. Wellingtons are essential. This was at one time the only remaining site in the British Isles. It has recently been discovered in Glamorgan.

Small Cudweed *Filago minima*
June to August.
Difficult to see whilst standing up – a hands and knees species.
Stoborough: on track 10m SE of and parallel to Soldiers Road – 75, 100 and 125m NE of S cattle grid. **Studland:** sandy area on W side of Ferry Road 250m N of entrance to Sewage Works; bank W of Visitor Centre; near paths N of car park N of Visitor Centre; 3.5Km N of village in Shell Bay car park.

Golden Samphire *Inula crithmoides*
July to August. *Nationally Scarce.*
Not related to edible Samphires, which are of two different families.
Tyneham: cliff at Pondfield beach. **Worth & Langton:** most cliff quarries. **Swanage:** sea end of gully E of Anvil Point; foot of cliff just above N end of Swanage promenade.

Chamomile *Chamaemelum nobile*
Mid June to September. *Dorset Scarce.*
A perennial species, which gives off a strong and pleasant aroma. It has narrow yellow scales in between the yellow disk florets, like the other Chamomiles, but which are lacking in Mayweeds.
Corfe: many areas on Corfe Common, especially along the NE side NW of B3069.

Lesser Water-plantain *Baldellia ranunculoides*
May to September. *Dorset Scarce.*
Stoborough: by pond by track 200m S of 'dd' on map in 'Middlebere
Heath'. **Corfe:** on edges of pond on Corfe Common by A351.

Italian Lords-and-ladies *Arum italicum* subsp. *neglectum*
Mid-May to mid-June (leaves from October). *Nationally Scarce.*
Poisonous. Leaves have narrow pale veins, and emerge in autumn,
making it easy to identify then: the leaves of Lords-and-ladies (*Arum
maculatum*) do not emerge until Christmas. Leaves of Italian Lords-and-
ladies mostly get covered in late spring by Bramble, Nettle etc. Few
flowers appear; most of those get damaged by slugs, snails, or birds.
Worth: on W side of Winspit path 300m N of Coast Path; at foot of
several Strip Lynchets in third field E of village. **Langton:** scattered
across steepest part of field above Dancing Ledge, some under bushes.
Swanage: E end of S-facing rocky escarpment N of Anvil Point
lighthouse (leaves late – perhaps they are hybrids).
(*Arum italicum* subsp *italicum*, with broader pale areas around the veins,
can be seen in five wild sites, but those are difficult to describe by

reference to the map. Site details are in *The Wild Flowers of The Isle of Purbeck, Brownsea and Sandbanks,* together with sites for garden escapes of the cultivated variety 'Marmoratum', or 'Pictum'.)

Marsh Helleborine *Epipactis palustris*
Late June to mid-July.
Look right into the flowers to appreciate their full beauty.
Kingston: 2.5Km S of village in wet hollows on sloping cliff NE of Egmont Bight – enter from Coast Path about halfway down W side of Houns-tout, and move around with care.

Autumn Lady's-tresses *Spiranthes spiralis*
Mid-August to mid-September. **Photo below left.**
The flowers are in a spiral. Numbers vary from year to year.
Church Knowle: widely and thinly scattered on Stonehill Down Nature
Reserve. **Corfe:** few on N side of Purbeck Way 150 to 325m W of radio
mast on Rollington Hill; 2.5Km E of village along S-facing top of
Brenscombe Hill on S of Purbeck Way for 500m. **Swanage:** W of Anvil
Point lighthouse; between Mile Indicator Posts; plentifully scattered
where "Studland Hill" is printed on map along 200m W to E.

Early Marsh Orchid *Dactylorhiza incarnata* subsp. *pulchella*
June. **Photo above right.**
Unlike the other subspecies of this Marsh Orchid, the sides of the lower
petal do not fold back until the floret has been out quite some time, and
sometimes not even then. The deep petal colour fades with age.
Stoborough: on Dismantled Tramway 250 to 300m N of A351. **Corfe:**
over 3Km N of village on W side of minor road to Slepe 200m S of N
cattle grid; in SW of small heath SW of Scotland. **Studland:** plentiful in
SE half of bog E of Ferry Road opposite bridleway to Greenlands (with
hybrids with Heath Spotted Orchid).

Early Spider Orchid *Ophrys sphegodes*
April to early May. *Nationally Scarce.* **See photo on front cover.**
This is the best area in Britain for this species. It is on the logo of the
Dorset Wildlife Trust. At a full count, in 2009, there were over 49,000
flowering. The plants are short-lived; half flower only once or twice.
They may enter a dormant phase of one, two, three or rarely more years
between flowering. About 50% of plants are dormant at any one time, so
a population will be about double the number flowering. The flower
spikes are usually under 10cm high here.
Worth: S of top of Coast Path steps on W side of Winspit cliff quarries.
Langton: many sloping fields by sea (including some flowers with
yellow frill to brown petal) – particularly plentiful in fields west and east
of field above Dancing Ledge. **Swanage:** scattered in Durlston Country
Park especially on the downs.

Wasp Orchid *Ophrys apifera* var. *trollii*
Mid-June.
Wasp Orchids have their lower petal narrowly V-shaped, with ground
colour pale (above left) or dark brown (above right), and, unlike Bee
Orchids, with their tip not bending backwards. This area is currently the
best in Britain for them. Each plant flowers only once.
Worth & Langton: Should be sought wherever there are Bee Orchids
on sloping fields above the sea, from the field W of Seacombe Quarry
(especially) to the field E of Dancing Ledge.

Finally, two of the wonderful displays of commoner flowers -

Wild Garlic (Ramsons) in Quarry Wood, Kingston, where it is a glorious sight in early May, as it is also in the wood SW of Tyneham village, Stonehill Down wood NW of Church Knowle, King's Wood W of Studland, and Studland Wood.

Kidney Vetch, by Old Harry Rocks – a marvellous sight in June.

Flowers and faith - a personal epilogue

In the nineteenth century most country parishes had their own clergyman. Some of them wrote about the flowers of their area as I have done. It seems appropriate to conclude with things I have learned of how The Bible uses flowers to illustrate truths.

The Bible tells me that God is creator. As I look into a flower, and examine the wonderful and beautiful detail of it, I am often moved to thank its designer. The account of creation also teaches me that God has put humans in charge of the Earth. We are called to conserve it.

Flowers remind me that my life on earth is temporary. "Man ... springs up like a flower and withers away." (From the book of Job). I need to be ready to meet God.

The wise men brought gifts, including myrrh, to the child Jesus. Myrrh was a spice made from a plant. It was used in burial. That gift foretold that Jesus' death would be significant. The Bible tells us that on the Cross he bore the sins of the world.

Jesus used illustrations. One of his stories is about a farmer's enemy sowing weeds among the wheat. Farm-workers asked to pull them up, but the farmer forbade them, until the harvest, in case they pulled up some of the wheat. He would have the weeds pulled first at harvest-time, and burnt, and then he would gather the wheat into his barn. This, Jesus said, was a picture of how God waits, until death, to separate those going to heaven from those who will perish.

Jesus also said that as a small seed grows into a tree, so his kingdom would grow. How true this has proved. Anyone who turns in repentance to follow Jesus Christ enters his kingdom.

My body is gradually wearing out. Writing to Christians at Corinth, the Apostle Paul used the illustration of a perishable seed (like our body) being sown, and so disappearing from view in the earth. Then a plant grows from it. Similarly, he says, after death God gives a Christian a new body, imperishable, fit for heaven. Praise God!

Index